FAST FORWARD

Volcanoes
Through Time

Published in 2009 by The Rosen Publishing Group, Inc.
29 East 21st Street, New York, NY 10010

Created and produced by Nicholas Harris and Claire Aston, Orpheus Books Ltd

U.S. editor: Kara Murray
Illustrator: Peter Dennis (*Linda Rogers Associates*)
Consultant: Susanna van Rose, writer and geologist

Library of Congress Cataloging-in-Publication Data

Harris, Nicholas.
Volcanoes through time / Nicholas Harris.
p. cm. — (Fast forward)
Includes index.
ISBN 978-1-4358-2800-1 (library binding)
1. Volcanoes—History—Juvenile literature. I. Title.
QE521.3.H248 2009
551.21—dc22

2008031680

Printed and bound in China

FAST FORWARD

Volcanoes
Through Time

illustrated by Peter Dennis

text by Nicholas Harris

PowerKiDS
press

New York

Contents

Introduction

Imagine you are in southern Italy thousands of years ago. The scene is dominated by a large volcano blasting ash into the air. One day the eruption will stop and calm will return. Then, many years down the road, a Roman city named Pompeii will be built on the plains beneath that same volcano, known as Vesuvius. The city is a picture of peace and wealth until one sunny August morning.

The story told in this book is like a journey. It is not a journey you can make by plane, car or ship. In fact, you don't have to go anywhere at all. You are about to travel through time. With each turn of the page, the date moves forward a few hours, days or years. You are still in the same place, but notice how many things change from one date to the next. Each time—each stop on your journey—is like a new chapter. The eruption, the falling pumice and ash, the blast that obliterated the city and the years that passed before the ruins were discovered all tell the story of Pompeii.

Use the thumb index to travel through time! This will help you make a quick comparison between one scene and another, even though some show events that took place many years apart. A little black arrow on the page points to the time of the scene illustrated on that page.

Vesuvius
erupting

6

25,000 Years Ago

Europe lies in the grip of the Ice Age. Vast ice sheets have spread out from the North Pole and the mountain ranges, concealing great expanses of land. Although ice has not come as far as southern Italy, the climate is cool and dry. Few trees grow here. Herds of saiga antelope graze the grasslands.

With a loud explosion, a volcano (which will one day be known as Vesuvius) erupts, blasting ash into the air. Alarmed by the shaking ground and deafening noise, the saiga gallop away, blocks of lava crashing all around them.

A cross-section of a volcano

Ash and lava layers laid down by earlier eruptions

A VOLCANO ERUPTS

A volcano is an opening in the Earth's crust, its rocky outer layer. (We usually think of a volcano as a cone-shaped mountain, but that is not always the case.) In a volcanic eruption, magma, hot melted rock from inside the Earth, is blasted out of the volcano's crater. It does this when gas that has built up inside the magma suddenly blows out. If the magma is thick and pasty, the eruption will be a very strong one. The erupted magma, called lava, is smashed into pumice and ash, forming a huge cloud. In lesser explosions, lava oozes from the crater and flows down the volcano's slopes.

Falling blocks of lava

Saiga galloping away from eruption

25,000 years ago

500 BC

Aug 24 AD 79 10 AM

Two hours later

One hour later

Later that afternoon

Early next morning

One year later

1250

1785

100 years later

Today

7

The Year 500 BC

The Ice Age has long been over. The summers in southern Italy are now warm and sunny. The soil is rich and crops grow very well. Vesuvius lies close by. It has not erupted for many centuries. The people who live here have no idea that it is a dangerous volcano. To them it is simply a cone-shaped hill.

One day, this land will be part of the great Roman Empire, but at this time it is under the rule of the Etruscans, a people from northern Italy.

Vesuvius

Italian pine trees

Farmhouse

Pigsty

Vines

8

VOLCANOES OF THE MEDITERRANEAN

The Earth's crust is like a jigsaw puzzle, divided into about 15 giant pieces scientists call tectonic plates. These plates are always moving, although usually too slowly for us to notice. Most volcanoes are found on or near the edges of these plates (these are also the places where most earthquakes occur). Some plate edges lie beneath the Mediterranean Sea.

THE BAY OF NAPLES

Above is a map of the Bay of Naples. The crater of Vesuvius is clearly seen. The bay has good harbors for sea-going ships and the land is very rich. For these reasons, this area has always had a large population. The towns of Pompeii and Herculaneum grew near the southern slopes of Vesuvius.

Etruscan temple

Plowing with oxen

25,000 years ago

500 BC

Aug 24 AD 79 10 AM

Two hours later

One hour later

Later that afternoon

Early next morning

One year later

1250

1785

100 years later

Today

9

August 24th AD 79 10 AM

It is a busy morning in the Roman town of Pompeii. In the square outside the temple people gather to buy their groceries. Yet something is wrong. Some of the animals are uneasy. A dog barks and strains at his leash. A donkey turns over the cart he is pulling, and a caged bird flaps around in a panic.

A farmer from the slopes of nearby Mount Vesuvius has noticed a bulge in the ground and felt a trembling underfoot. He hurries down to Pompeii to tell everyone what he has seen.

Vesuvius

Arch of Caligula

IMP · CAESAR · DIV · GERMANICVS

Writing messages

Bar

Drawing water

THE ROMANS

In the first century AD, most of Europe was under the rule of the Romans. Over many centuries Rome had grown from a small settlement on the banks of the River Tiber, in Italy, to the capital of a vast empire. The surrounding region became rich, able to trade in peace under the protection of the Roman army.

Prosperous towns such as Pompeii grew close to the Bay of Naples, 124 miles (200 km) southeast of Rome. A busy harbor brought in ships full of goods from overseas. Wealthy Pompeii merchants traded wine, cloth and *garum* (a fish sauce) for glassware, precious stones and spices. People crowded the town's bars and shops.

FORTVNAE A

Temple of Fortuna Augusta

Butchers

Market stall

Guard

11

25,000 years ago

500 BC

Aug 24 AD 79 10 AM

Two hours later

One hour later

Later that afternoon

Early next morning

One year later

1250

1785

100 years later

Today

Two Hours Later...

Suddenly, there is a deafening explosion. Everyone in the square turns to look up at Vesuvius. People about to sit down to their midday meal indoors rush out onto the streets. Everyone stands and stares, spellbound by a shocking sight.

At just after noon, the buildup of gases finally blew out the magma in Vesuvius' crater. The volcano erupted, blasting a column of pumice and ash (powdered volcanic rock) more than 12 miles (20 km) straight up into the air.

This is what the eruption of Vesuvius would have looked like. The cloud of ash and pumice is shot high into the air before it spreads out.

Vesuvius

IMP·CAESAR·DIV·GERMANICVS

Arch of Caligula

People watching eruption

Shooting up into the air from the mountain's top is a dense, black cloud. The people of Pompeii gasp in shock. Few guessed that "their" mountain was actually a volcano. What they do not realize is that the eruption will soon put their lives in great danger. Some remember the great earthquake of 17 years earlier and wonder whether their houses will be damaged once again.

FORTVNAE A

Temple of Fortuna Augusta

Market stall

Guard

25,000 years ago

500 BC

Aug 24 AD 79 10 AM

Two hours later

One hour later

Later that afternoon

Early next morning

One year later

1250

1785

100 years later

Today

13

The cloud of pumice that erupted from Vesuvius reached its greatest height after about an hour. Winds then began to blow it southeast across Pompeii. The pumice then began to fall on the city.

One Hour Later...

Pumice starts to rain down on Pompeii. The small pieces are too light to wound anyone seriously, but some people protect their heads anyway. The children discover pumice is good for sliding on, but some adults slip on it.

Lightning

Vesuvius

Arch of Caligula

IMP · CAESAR · DIV · GERMANICVS

Head protection

Sliding on pumice

Meanwhile, the eruption continues. The cloud has now started to spread out toward Pompeii. Some people who watch the eruption from farther away later describe the shape of this cloud as similar to that of an Italian pine tree *(see page 8)*. The sky darkens and lightning flashes in the gathering gloom.

Pumice and ash settle on the ground. It will continue to fall for 19 hours.

FORTVNAE A

Temple of Fortuna Augusta

Market stall

Guard

25,000 years ago

500 BC

Aug 24 AD 79 10 AM

Two hours later

One hour later

Later that afternoon

Early next morning

One year later

1250

1785

100 years later

Today

15

This is what volcanic ash looks like under a microscope. The specks range in size from sand to flour. They are the remains of walls of bubbles inside the magma. These were caused by gas escaping from inside the liquid rock as it turned into pumice *(see page 7)*.

Later That Afternoon...

The pumice and ash lie on the ground about 3 feet (1 m) thick. Many roofs have started to fall in under the weight. People realize that their houses are in danger of falling down and that they are no longer safe inside. Panic sets in.

Many people gather up their belongings, tie pillows to their heads to protect themselves from falling rocks and flee Pompeii. It is already too late to use a cart as the wheels become stuck in the pumice, so people carry what they can and walk through the streets.

Arch of Caligula

IMP·CAESAR·DIV·GERMANICVS

People fleeing city

Cart stuck in pumice and ash

16

A dog, chained up and forgotten by its owner, barks wildly, straining at its leash. The guard, as instructed by his commanding officer, remains dutifully at his post.

Some people decide to stay. Many are too afraid to take to the streets. They pray to the gods that the dreadful fall of powdery rock will stop soon.

Roof collapsing under weight of pumice

Temple of Fortuna Augusta

Dog on leash

Pumice and ash lying thick on ground

Guard

17

25,000 years ago

500 BC

Aug 24 AD 79 10 AM

Two hours later

One hour later

Later that afternoon

Early next morning

One year later

1250

1785

100 years later

Today

This illustration shows the collapse of the column of ash and pumice and the beginning of the pyroclastic flow that covered Pompeii.

Not all volcanic eruptions are as severe as Vesuvius in AD 79. Sometimes, runny lava squirts out of a crack in the ground.

Early Next Morning...

The new day dawns in murky darkness. There is a loud explosion. A glowing red cloud rolls alarmingly down the slopes of Vesuvius toward Pompeii. The few people that remain in the city look on in horror. What is this new danger?

Suddenly a blast of hot air knocks them off their feet. The force is so powerful it causes stone columns to crash to the ground. Soon afterward, an avalanche of hot ash streams into the city, smashing almost everything in its path. Pompeii is destroyed.

Marble breaks off arch

IMP. CAESAR. DIV. GERMANICVS.

Glowing cloud

Hot air blast knocks people over

GLOWING AVALANCHES

It was once thought that Pompeii was simply buried beneath layers of pumice and ash. Now there is proof that avalanches of rock, glowing and red hot, flowed down the slopes of Vesuvius and destroyed the city. Scientists call these avalanches pyroclastic flows (the word "pyroclastic" means "fractured by fire"). They happen when the great cloud of ash and pumice that blasts into the sky after a volcano erupts *(see page 12)* collapses back down to earth. Scientists studying a recent volcanic eruption (Mount St. Helens, United States, in 1980) discovered that a pyroclastic flow could travel at speeds of up to 185 miles per hour (300 km/h).

Temple collapsing

19

25,000 years ago

500 BC

Aug 24 AD 79 10 AM

Two hours later

One hour later

Later that afternoon

Early next morning

One year later

1250

1785

100 years later

Today

Because volcanic rock is so soft, it can be very easily dug out. This illustration shows the rock churches of Cappadocia, in southern Turkey. The layers of ash, mud and lava created by ancient volcanic eruptions have been worn away over the centuries, leaving isolated pillars. People discovered that the rock could be hollowed out to provide shelters. About a thousand years ago, many churches were dug out of the rocks.

During the eruption, Vesuvius really did "blow its top." The force of the explosion blasted apart the peak of the volcano. A vast new crater, measuring nearly 2 miles (4 km) across, was created.

One Year Later...

Where there was once a city of 20,000 people, surrounded by rich fields and vineyards, now there is a barren landscape.

Vesuvius

Ravine

Nothing grows here. The only people are curious visitors. Everywhere there is a thick layer of gray "snow," the ash and pumice that fell on Pompeii during the eruption of Vesuvius. It is between 10 and 15 feet (3-5 m) deep, completely covering the ruins of the Roman city.

Each time it rains, rushing streams flow, gouging out ravines in the soft matter. A few bare tree stumps stick out above the ash layers.

Yet within a few years, the countryside will be rich and green once more. Volcanic soils are very rich, and plants and flowers soon burst into life.

Barren, ash-covered ground

Ravine

Hunting party

Tree stumps

21

25,000 years ago

500 BC

Aug 24 AD 79 10 AM

Two hours later

One hour later

Later that afternoon

Early next morning

One year later

1250

1785

100 years later

Today

The illustrations show how the shape of Vesuvius has changed over the centuries. The first *(above)* shows what it probably looked like just before the AD 79 eruption.

This is the crater of Vesuvius immediately after the eruption. The top has been blown off by the explosion.

Today, a new cone has formed on the south side of the old crater. It has erupted many times since AD 79.

Volcanoes grow out of the ground. Sometimes they can reach a great height in just a few years. On Vesuvius, a new volcanic cone began to grow over the centuries. There was still magma underneath it.

More Than 1,000 Years Later...

Lying under its thick blanket of volcanic ash and pumice, Pompeii has been buried and forgotten for many years. The Roman Empire also ended

Vesuvius

Gold coin

Finding broken tiles

many centuries ago, and no new cities have been settled in this area. Instead, country people plow the land and graze their livestock. The rich volcanic soil ensures that their farms are successful, and they live good lives.

Sometimes, coins, tiles, pieces of pottery or old columns are dug up, but no one thinks anything of them.

THE STORY OF VESUVIUS

Vesuvius has erupted about 80 times since AD 79, although rarely with such devastating power. The worst eruption was in 1631, when 4,000 people were killed. Glowing avalanches were, once again, the cause of this disaster.

The last time Vesuvius erupted was in 1944. Since then, it has been dormant (inactive between eruptions). No one knows when it might erupt again or how powerful that eruption might be.

A volcano that has stopped erupting altogether is described as extinct. Since there may be many hundreds of years between eruptions, it is often hard to decide whether a volcano is extinct or not.

Old column

23

25,000 years ago

500 BC

Aug 24 AD 79 10 AM

Two hours later

One hour later

Later that afternoon

Early next morning

One year later

1250

1785

100 years later

Today

The discovery of the lost cities of Pompeii and Herculaneum began with finds of pieces of marble with inscriptions carved on them. Here, a peasant comes across such a find while digging a well in the ground. Some earlier discoveries that even had the name of Pompeii inscribed on them were overlooked.

The ruins of Pompeii were captivating to many artists. Soon after Pompeii was found, some made careful drawings of the remains.

The Year 1785

Wealthy people from all over Europe visit the ruins of Pompeii. Ever since the news broke that an ancient city had been discovered under the ground near Vesuvius, travelers have been eager to see the remains for themselves.

Some of Pompeii's visitors are treasure hunters, with wheelbarrows and shovels. Pieces of marble are broken off and taken away as souvenirs.

Vesuvius

Digging for treasure

Columns, pots, statues and wall paintings are dug up and taken away. Some discoveries are used as ornaments. Others are put on display in museums.

But other people come to study the ruins in order to find out about the past. They make drawings and try to imagine what Pompeii's buildings would have looked like before they were destroyed.

THE DISCOVERY OF POMPEII

The lost city of Pompeii remained forgotten for many centuries. Even after the ruins of buildings, statues and wall paintings were discovered by workmen building a tunnel in 1594, nobody was interested. In 1710 a peasant digging a well a few miles (km) from where Pompeii once stood found several blocks of marble buried deep in the ground. Then a local nobleman guessed that other treasures might be found there and bought the land. The remains of old houses were dug up and Herculaneum, another town destroyed in the AD 79 eruption of Vesuvius, was soon discovered. It was not long before people came across the ruins of Pompeii. Digging began in 1748.

25,000 years ago

500 BC

Aug 24 AD 79 10 AM

Two hours later

One hour later

Later that afternoon

Early next morning

One year later

1250

1785

100 years later

Today

Finding a statue

Column

25

A Hundred Years Later...

Thanks to the efforts of hundreds of workers armed with picks and shovels, the ruins of Pompeii are gradually appearing from the deep layers of pumice and ash that have covered them over for so long. An archaeologist called Giuseppe Fiorelli has been appointed to supervise the excavation of Pompeii. He has made sure that proper scientific records are made of Pompeii's ruins.

First of all, mounds of ash are cleared away. He divides up the location into

Vesuvius

Carrying away rubble in baskets

Arch of Caligula (brick arch stripped of marble)

Removing ash

Supervisor

Photographer

regions. Every block and building inside each region is given a number. This means that whenever an object is found, its exact position can be recorded. Now scientists can find out much more about how people lived in Roman times.

Teams of workers (some are prisoners) carry away pumice and ash in straw baskets, watched over by supervisors. They make sure nothing is stolen. Other workers make plaster casts of dead people whose skeletons have been found. They were the unfortunate ones who could not escape the glowing avalanches that engulfed Pompeii *(see page 18)*. The layers of volcanic ash that covered them over quickly hardened. In time, the flesh and clothing rotted away, leaving body-shaped hollows in the ash. Giuseppe Fiorelli invented a way of making copies of the bodies by pouring plaster into these hollows.

25,000 years ago

500 BC

Aug 24 AD 79 10 AM

Two hours later

One hour later

Later that afternoon

Early next morning

One year later

1250

1785

100 years later

Today

Making plaster casts

Supervisor

Artist

Statue

27

The finds made at Pompeii tell us a great deal about life in Roman times. By being buried in ash, even some foods have lasted to the present day.

Fiorelli's method of making plaster casts was also used for animals. This dog was buried alive, struggling to free itself from its chain.

Contests between gladiators were popular in Roman times. There was an amphitheater (a kind of stadium) in Pompeii where such contests took place. Wall paintings, plaster casts of gladiators' bodies and finds of helmets and armor tell us what the contests were like.

Today

Visitors flock to see the ruins of Pompeii (about two million come each year). There are guides on hand to make sure that people can find their way around the streets. They also answer questions about, for example, what life was like in Pompeii before it was destroyed, what happened during the eruption of Vesuvius and how the ruins were discovered and restored for all to see.

The ruins of ancient Pompeii are very old and need to be looked after carefully.

Vesuvius

Arch of Caligula

Guide

Well

28

At the mercy of the weather and pollution, the crumbling walls are at risk of falling into a worse condition.

Many of Pompeii's tall buildings were knocked down by the great force of the glowing avalanches *(see page 18)*. Some of those that have remained standing were seized for building stone a long time ago. As a result, tall buildings are quite rare in Pompeii, although the great Arch of Caligula still stands proudly.

The visitors take in the many wonderful sights Pompeii still boasts. They wander around its streets enjoying the warm, sunny weather. Some wonder what it would be like to live and work in Pompeii when it was an active Roman town nearly 2,000 years ago.

Have you noticed how some people in this scene remind you of characters that appeared here in Roman times? Take a close look on pages 10 and 11!

25,000 years ago

500 BC

Aug 24 AD 79 10 AM

Two hours later

One hour later

Later that afternoon

Early next morning

One year later

1250

1785

100 years later

Today

Ruins of Temple of Fortuna Augusta

Kiosk

Guard

29 ▶

Glossary

amphitheater (AMP-fuh-thee-uh-ter) In Roman times, an oval-shaped building used for gladiatorial contests. It had a central stage surrounded by rows of seats rising above it.

archaeologist (ahr-kee-AH-luh-jist) Someone who studies human life in the past, using the evidence from finds buried in the ground or at sea.

crater (KRAY-tur) The circular, funnel-shaped basin at the top of a volcanic cone.

dormant volcano (DOR-ment vol-KAY-noh) A volcano that has stopped erupting, but that may burst into life again.

earthquake (URTH-kwayk) A shaking or trembling of the ground, caused by the sudden movement of part of the Earth's crust. Earthquakes usually (but not always) occur near the boundaries of tectonic plates.

eruption (ih-RUP-shun) The blasting out of lava, ash or pumice from a volcano into the air or onto the Earth's surface.

excavation (ek-skuh-VAY-shun) The unearthing of buried objects in an attempt to find out about the past.

extinct volcano (ek-STINKT vol-KAY-noh) A volcano that has stopped erupting forever.

gladiators (GLA-dee-ay-turz) In Roman times, men trained to fight for public entertainment.

Ice Age (YS AYJ) A cold period in the Earth's history when ice spreads out from the poles and mountain ranges to cover large areas of the Earth's surface. The last Ice Age began about 2 million years ago.

inscriptions (in-SKRIP-shunz) Writing carved on wood, stone or metal.

magma (MAG-muh) Hot, melted (molten) rock that comes from beneath the solid rock of the Earth's crust.

plaster cast (PLAS-ter KAST) A copy or form of a person, animal or object made from plaster of Paris, a white powder that sets to a hard solid when mixed with water.

pumice (PUH-mus) A volcanic glass "froth" formed from cooling gassy lava. It has many bubbles.

ruins (ROO-enz) Old, falling-down buildings.

tectonic plates (tek-TO-nik PLAYTS) The large pieces into which the Earth's surface is divided. Each plate moves slowly, either pushing into another plate, sliding underneath it or pulling away from it. Many volcanoes are located at or near the plate boundaries.

volcanic ash (vol-KA-nik ASH) Lava that has been blown to powder by the force of the explosion when a volcano erupts.

pyroclastic flow (py-roh-KLAS-tik FLOH) Hot, glowing avalanches of lava pieces that stream down the slopes of the volcano during an eruption.

ravine (ruh-VEEN) A deep, narrow valley formed by the action of a fast-running stream.

Index

Web Sites

Due to the changing nature of Internet links, PowerKids Press has developed an online list of Web sites related to the subject of this book. This site is updated regularly. Please use this link to access the list:
www.powerkidslinks.com/fastfor/volcano/